From Tragedy to Triumph!

by Vange Anderson

PublishAmerica
Baltimore

First printing

PublishAmerica has allowed this work to remain exactly as the author intended, verbatim, without editorial input.

Hardcover 978-1-4512-4320-8
Softcover 978-1-60749-090-6
Pocketbook 978-1-4512-8436-2
PUBLISHED BY PUBLISHAMERICA, LLLP
www.publishamerica.com
Baltimore

Printed in the United States of America

Dedicated to our Amy

*In her loving memory and in the blessed hope
of seeing her again…*

Acknowledgments

It takes a village to raise a child. The same is true of a book. So many people have encouraged me along the way, and I am thankful for each and every one.

My first thanks go to God. I don't even want to think about where I'd be without Him. He held me up, healed me and encouraged me to grow closer to the image he has for me. His love is unconditional. Thank you Father, Lord Jesus Christ, and thank you, Holy Spirit. Any praise and honor for this book should go directly to You.

My husband, Dick: You've been my best friend for over 30 years now. I treasure the encouraging words you can speak to my heart with just a certain look in your eyes. Thank you for believing in me and for loving me "in the midst of it all". I am so thankful you're a man of God. Your faith shines through your words and actions. Thank you for the gift of who you are.

Our precious children: Mark, Mary, Bob and Jeff. Mark, you got me through things I didn't think I'd survive. You are so precious to my heart and I am so proud of you. Mary, oh my

Mary, you could talk about your sister with me when no one else in the family could. You helped keep me sane and have blessed me in ways you don't even know about. Bob, the love I see in your eyes blesses me beyond words. Your ability to take my manuscript and edit it was awesome. It can't be easy to correct your mother's work, but you did it graciously. Thank you. And Jeffrey John, your name means "God's gracious gift of peace", and so you are. You bring peace to my world every time you say, "Hello, Lady". You have given me wonderful insights by your care and concern for others. All of you make me smile with my heart. Without your love, I'm not sure I would have had the courage to go on. Thank you for the gift of who you are. I am one blessed mom!

Jack Reynolds and Gina Bernard: Both of you encouraged me in the beginning of my work, correcting my punctuation, making suggestions that made the manuscript better. May the kindness you extended to me be returned to you ten-fold. Your willingness to help an aspiring writer encouraged me to complete my work. Thank you.

The staff at PublishAmerica.: Your replies to my questions were always speedy. I seemed to make a connection with several of you—to the point that if we were neighbors, we would also be friends. Thank you for your professionalism as well as your friendliness and encouragement.

And to the dear lady from the Washington D.C. area who prayed over me and gave me the title to my book. Thank you. You have blessed me. May you in turn be blessed.

There are many who helped in the writing of this book just by being part of my story. To my faithful prayer warriors, I stand amazed at your faithfulness. There were times when I asked God to wake you up in the middle of the night to pray. I have no doubt that you did just that. To those who visited me when I was grieving: Your presence spoke volumes to me. I am reminded that as you did it to the least of these, His servants, you did it unto Him. As you treated me, you treated Jesus through me. Thank you for showing me His love.

Whether your names are included in this account or not, your names are dear to my heart and I thank God for your presence in my life.

Table of Contents

From Tragedy
to Triumph!

Introduction

It is with both sadness and joy that I write this. Sadness, for the loss of our daughter, joy, for the hope of seeing her again.

As Christians we are not immune from tragedy, disease, or any kind of difficult problem. On the contrary, God has told us that we will have troubles in this world, but to "be of good cheer for He has overcome the world" (John 16:33). Though we may encounter problems, we need to remember that "He is bigger than any problem we will ever encounter and that He is faithful and will lead us through" (Ps. 50:15, Ps. 46:1

It may be that it is in our trials that we find out who we truly are. We are God's children and He is our Abba Daddy who is faithful, never leaves us, and can be relied on to hold us up (Heb. 13:5, Romans 8:16)

Consider what he tells us in the Bible. In Psalms 34:18, we are told: "The Lord is near to the brokenhearted." And in Proverbs 3:5b-6: "Lean not on your own understanding, but in all your ways acknowledge him and he shall direct thy paths."

I'm so thankful for His promises, and have leaned heavily on them in times of struggle.

Admittedly, there are still days when I struggle, but that's normal. However, the times when I focus more on the future are more frequent. Some day I will see Amy again! She is in my future, and that is enough to cause my heart to rejoice. I hope you will join me in a struggle that brought me to that point: from tragedy to triumph.

Our Amy was a wonderful 17-year-old girl who had time for the young and old. The children at church loved her because she was one of the only teenagers who would pay any attention to them. Once a week she stayed with her aging grandmother to take care of her. She would get her up in the middle of the night, take her to the bathroom, clean her up, and get her back to bed. At seventeen I wouldn't have been able to do that, but Amy did. If she saw me feeling down, she would either nudge her dad to give me a hug, or come to me herself, saying, "Mom, you look like you could use a hug." Then she would place her arms on my shoulders and just grin. Oh, how I miss her.

After the accident that took her, I came face-to-face with the grief a parent deals with upon the loss of a child. God met me at my point of need immediately, providing me with numbness to delay the pain, alerting groups of intercessors to surround me with protective and healing prayer, and girding me with the faith I needed to get through that horrible experience.

He has also shown me many things through the ensuing months and years: his comfort, hope, love; his counsel and ability to change my focus from despair to hope. He taught me lessons I'm deeply grateful for but wish I had never learned. For if I had never learned them, my daughter would still be here. Getting through grief for your child is a huge struggle, one you can't truly imagine unless you've been through it yourself.

I believe God met Amy at her point of need too. I believe He was there, or at least sent his angels to minister to her in her hour of need. She didn't suffer, and for that I'm very grateful, but missing her has become a normal part of my existence. In the years since the accident, there hasn't been one solitary day when I didn't think of her.

My prayer is that you will find comfort and hope in the following pages, and that you will take the ideas presented and apply them to your own situation. May what you read here help you minister to others more effectively and give the glory to God more earnestly; for it is to his glory that we are able to function with hope for the future.

May God give you the guidance and insight to apply this story to your own life; and may he bless you in his abundant, incredible love for you. Blessings to you, my unseen friend! May God give you the peace you seek.

Chapter 1
The Accident

"For I am persuaded, that neither death, nor life, nor angels, nor principalities, nor powers, nor things present, nor things to come, nor height, nor depth, nor any other creature, shall be able to separate us from the love of God, which is in Christ Jesus our Lord."—Romans 8:37-39

God gives us numbness to allow us to function when on our own power we would fall apart. After the accident I operated on 'automatic pilot' for quite some time.

July 3, 2000, started out to be a lovely day. Our children had just come home from a campout and were playing hackey-sack in the yard. Glancing out the window, I thought how nice it was that Amy was joining in the game with her brothers and sister. How glad I was she had gone camping with them and was finally growing into her role as grown-up sister, included in their activities. Watching her play made me smile.

Later on that afternoon she asked if she could go on a pre-July 4th outing with her friend. Standing in the yard with them,

I said my usual parting words to her: "You'll have a better time if you get a hug and a kiss from your mom before you go." I hugged her, gave her a kiss, and told her I loved her. She said, "I love you too, Mom." And then she was gone.

Some time later I was weeding the flowers and bushes in front of our house. A police car drove into our driveway, and our nephew Tim (a volunteer fireman) told us Amy had been in an accident and that it was bad. He directed us to the hospital.

The accident site was about a half mile from the T in the road. We turned left; the accident site was to the right. As we drove down that road I had an uncanny feeling we were driving away from Amy. In truth, we were. The emergency personnel were still working on her. I'm sure our presence there would have been upsetting to everyone, including us. However, part of me wanted to be there to hold her, to give her whatever comfort I could, to encourage her to fight to hold on and stay with us.

In the private room close to the ER, we waited. I called some friends to put Amy on their prayer chains, my brother and sister to let them know what happened. We waited and waited, crying out to our to God and pleading for Amy to hold on.

Finally, a nurse came and directed my husband Dick and me into the trauma room. The moment I walked in there, I knew she was gone. My first thought was, "Oh, honey, you're not in there." My first audible words were, "Oh, honey, reach out to Jesus. Reach out to Jesus." The emergency crew was still working on her and while I knew their work was for our benefit, I didn't want them to stop. I didn't want to hear the words that would make it real. I stroked Amy's right leg below the knee—back and forth, back and forth. Oh Lord, don't let this be real.

After a minute or two, the doctor, who was standing right next to me massaging Amy's heart, said, "We have not gotten any response at all. It is time for us to stop." I nodded my head, not in agreement, but in understanding of what he said. I'll never forget the look in his blue eyes nor the expression on his face. What a difficult thing that must be to have to tell a mother.

Two of our other children, Mary and Jeff, were then called into the trauma room. Jeffrey, bless his heart, kept asking Amy not to leave him and sat next to her the entire time we were there. Mary checked some medical signs (she is now a P.A.) and knew her sister would never have been the same. Their evident love for their sister blessed me and broke my heart at the same time.

I was surprised as other friends and relatives came into the trauma room. I don't know how they found out, but they came to support us and to grieve in those first horrible hours. Our priest came and we all gathered around our precious Amy and prayed those precious prayers for her soul. One of my friends who is a born again Evangelical later told me it was one of the most holy and reverential experiences she had ever had. Her words still carry a blessing to my soul.

Going to the registration desk, I signed the papers so the insurance papers could be filed. A woman from church was working the desk that night. Seeing her somehow made the ordeal do-able. I was thankful for her presence. Weird thing to say, but I was comforted. She was familiar and everything that was happening was alien. Somehow she brought a sense of order to the chaos.

It must be very difficult to ask a newly grieving parent if they would like to donate body tissues of someone they love so dearly. Amazingly, it was a question we had recently discussed. A month or two earlier, Amy had talked about donating her organs if anything ever happened to her. We knew by the smile on her face that we would honor her by doing that, so we did. The fact that I've always considered our physical bodies to be our "apartments" while on Earth also made that decision easier…not easy. No. Never. Just "easier".

The caring hospital personnel allowed us to stay with Amy for quite some time. Finally, they said they would need to begin working on her in order to salvage her organs and body tissues. Reluctantly, yet in relief, we left the hospital.

It was now dark outside, and dark in our hearts. It was a somber drive home, everyone in quiet thoughts of their own. When we walked into our house, two dear neighbors were there to meet us. Pastor Mark and Bruce didn't want us to walk into an empty house, so they waited there with open arms. Pastor Mark came to me saying, "Oh, Honey." His tears said it all. His prayer was a simple: "Oh, Jesus. Oh, Jesus." For me, that said it all. Only Jesus. Oh, how we needed Him now.

Chapter 2
Getting Everyone Together

*"In all thy ways acknowledge him,
and he shall direct thy paths."*—Proverbs 3:6

Getting everyone together doesn't sound like a tough assignment, but it can be. Our son Bob was on his honeymoon in Europe, at the moment on a cruise on the Mediterranean Sea. Just getting a hold of him was a major problem. Trying several times, the response was always, "No speak English. Call back nine."

Finally our friend John worked through the military and was able to get someone out to the ship to inform Bob. It was about three in the morning when Bob called home. My heart broke for him so far from home. Oh, how I wanted to hold him in my arms. My arms just weren't long enough.

The next day Bob called to say he could get a flight to Germany and another to Chicago, but could not get connections from there to Minneapolis, nor could they get another one home. That is where the Lord stepped in and provided the help we needed…directing the path to get Bob home!

Our oldest son, Mark, works on the cutting edge of computer technology. (There isn't a thing I do on the computer that impresses him!) Jack is a wonderful communicator, and Craig is excellent in both areas. I have no doubt that God arranged for the three of them to work together. Jack was on the phone talking to airline personnel. They told him there were absolutely no seats available on any flights from Chicago to Minneapolis nor from Minneapolis home in the time frame we needed. Mark and Craig, who were searching for flights on the computer, found the needed flights. Mark told Jack, "Yes, there are. Tell them to check flight number…" Their response was, "Oh, You're right," and the flights home were arranged.

Thank you, Lord! Thank you for arranging for these men to be in one place so they could work through this problem! It was exactly what we needed! (Of course, we thanked the men as well!)

Our family went en masse to the airport to pick Bob up. We walked in the door at the exact moment they were walking out the door from their flight. And yes, I was the first one to grab Bobby and wrap my arms around him! How good it felt to finally hold him close!

It was at that point he gave me a gift, saying, "We bought this for Amy while we were in Europe. I think she would want you to have it." Bless his heart, I didn't think I would be able to handle it without breaking down. When I looked at it, however, I saw that it was wrapped in duct tape.

Strange as it may sound, the sight of that tape is what

allowed me to cope. Duct taped packages are something of a joke in our family…a lot of tape to create a challenging package to open, a package wrapped in "love." Seeing it was enough to break the tension. It made me smile…as if it was a gift prepared just for me with love. I even wondered if Amy was smiling down at all of us, giving us her blessing, even laughing at all the tape that was used just for me.

Isn't that just like God? He knew I would have to open the package and made sure it was wrapped in duct tape so my spirits would be lifted at the exact moment of need. Awesome.

Chapter 3
Numb Is Good

"Fear thou not; for I am with thee: be not dismayed; for I am thy God: I will strengthen thee; yea, I will help thee; yea, I will uphold thee with the right hand of my righteousness."
—Isaiah 41:10

Yes, God helps us stand up by giving us numbness. That is what allowed me to function in a world that seemed to be falling apart. Did I say "seemed to be"? Correction, *was* falling apart.

Making arrangements for your child's funeral should never have to be done. They can do it for us, but we shouldn't have to do it for them. It's not the right order, it's backwards; it turns your world upside-down. There is nothing fair about it. But we weren't promised fair; we were just promised a "very present help in trouble' (Psalm 46:1).

Numbness dulls the pain we're not yet able to experience. It's one of the ways God protects us. I'm thankful for that. Numbness gave me time to gather strength, feel the prayers of the faithful lifting me up, experience the love of loved ones, friends, neighbors, and people I didn't even know. It gave me time to walk through the preparations we had to make, time before the realization of the permanence of her absence sunk in.

Whenever Kevin, our dear funeral director, asked how I was doing, my response was always the same, "Numb is good." I was on automatic pilot…going through the motions, not feeling the depth of pain that was to come.

I knew in my head what had happened, but my heart hadn't figured it out, and I hoped it never would. I was afraid the pain would be too great. (Oh, me of little faith. I should know my God will provide the strength when I need it, not before.)

Numbness is just one of the ways God protects us. He has many ways of protection that we take for granted. Ways we do not always attribute to him: friends that show up in a time of need, people notified to pray, the right people on hand to perform a particular task, and so on. He's the great designer, the infinitely creative creator. The One who is always with us and ready to help (what an awesome vision of him that is).

Chapter 4
Affirmation of Faith

"…and Jesus saith unto them, Believe ye that I am able to do this?" They said unto him, Yea, Lord."—Matthew 9:28

The Bible has been called "The Good News". It proclaims, "…he hath sent me to heal the brokenhearted" (Luke 4:18, KJV). And He does! How precious is that promise. The reaffirmation of my faith was a very important step.

One night as I was lying in bed I heard the words, "Well, do you still believe in me?" My response, thank God (literally), was, "To whom would I go? You have the words of everlasting life" (John 6:68).

I didn't realize it until years later, but that was the first step in my healing process. Did I still believe in God after the unthinkable happened? When my precious daughter would no longer rest her arms on my shoulders and say, "You look like you need a hug." Did I really still believe and trust in God?

It surprised me that I never expressed anger at God. My thinking at the time was, "How can I be mad at God when He's the one who was ministering to my daughter when I couldn't?" He was there, meeting her at her point of need, just as he was here, meeting me at mine. He was the only one who could help her transition from this world to the next. How could I be mad at him for that? It seemed ludicrous to me to be angry at him.

Therefore, I wouldn't allow myself to express anger at God. Oh, to be sure, if I had had a premonition about the accident, I would have nailed Amy to the floor to prevent it. There was no premonition. (At the time, I did not recognize the lack of a premonition as a reason to be angry at God, but later found out I really was angry at Him for not warning me.)

I always said I would trade places with Amy in a heartbeat, and I would. But then, I would be in heaven and she would be grieving. That doesn't sound like a very loving thing to do either. Frustration permeated my soul; but express anger at God when he was helping us? Unthinkable.

From time to time the thought of anger at God did surface in my mind. However, I always stuffed it back down. I questioned myself in terms of how could I be mad at God when He helped Amy when no one else could? I'm not immune from tragedy. God has told me I WILL have troubles.

How could I be angry at someone who told me I would have problems in this world but promised to be with me and lead me through it? He can be relied on to hold me up. He was taking care of Amy in heaven. Could I express anger for that? Absolutely not.

Ah, but there was one day a couple of years later…when I was having a quiet time with the Lord. I heard, "You know…part of you is mad at me." I said, "Yeah, you're probably right." Did you notice that faith-filled word, "probably"? Probably? Oh, come on. He's God. Of course he's right.

It was only then that I faced the reality of my anger at God. I did not face it well nor did I face it fully. But at least it was acceptable. I began to acknowledge the fact that. yes, I was angry that he hadn't protected her from the accident itself. Other people had come through accidents with no major injuries. Why not my daughter? People have prayed for victims of accidents and miraculous healings have occurred. Why not for my daughter? Why, when she was just coming into herself and realizing she had gifts and talents to share? Why, when she was so young and had her whole life ahead of her? Why...when we loved her so much? Why, why?

The fact that I was even asking the questions amazed me. I had never gotten into the "why" of her death. There isn't an answer to that "why" that would ever be good enough for me, so why ask? I would have argued with every one of the answers; with the possible exception that it kept her from going through something worse. And I probably would have argued about that too… "You could have kept her from that as well."

We serve a God who is strong enough and loves us enough to handle our anger and frustration with him. And if we can't face the fact of our anger, he is loving and gentle enough to wait until we can. He will let us know when the time is right. He knows all about our thoughts and feelings anyway, so we might as well be honest with Him. Thankfully, at last, I was able to be honest with Him.

Chapter 5
Comforting Vision

"Blessed are they that mourn; for they shall be comforted."
—Matthew 5:4

After Amy's death I experienced a vision that was incredibly comforting to me. Since it was also unsettling, I hesitated to share it with anyone. I thought they'd think I was losing it. I was afraid they would deny me the reality of my experience (and the comfort it provided) by telling me God doesn't work that way anymore.

At the end of that first month, my daughter Mary and I spent an afternoon at Art in the Park. On our way out I noticed some of Amy's friends working in a food booth and thought, "Oh, honey. You should be there." And there she was.

It happened just like it would in the movies. The scene as it actually was disappeared and in its place was a larger-than-life vision of my precious Amy. An oval image, it had a hazy light brown frame, about 12 inches wide. Amy was almost as tall as the tree behind the vision (the very top of which I could still see). A gorgeous smile was on her face, her hair was curled under, just above her shoulders, and she had on her favorite outfit (blue jeans, and a blue Nike shirt, with the white checkmark on the front). Her arms were at her side and she was sunlit from behind. With that gorgeous smile and love in her eyes she said, "Hi, Mom."

Thinking I was going to lose it right there in Art in the Park, I turned to go. Instantly regretting that move and wanting to gaze at her as long as possible, I turned around. The vision was gone. I felt horrible about that for the longest time. Did I hurt her feelings by turning away from her? Did she know I was sorry? I longed to hug her and tell her I was sorry…to tell her how much I loved her…to express appreciation for seeing her in that vision. But of course, that was impossible. The only thing I could do was ask God to tell her for me, and so I did. Eventually I came to think of my turning away as a gift because I didn't see the vision fade. It is as clear to me today as the wondrous moment I was allowed to see it.

The vision had lasted only several seconds, but in that time I was assured that my precious daughter was all right. She's in a wonderful place we call heaven. She's happy. Her gorgeous smile told me that. She's wearing her favorite outfit and feels right at home. If she had the chance to come back I don't think she would. It's too wonderful there. No pain, no sorrow. I think she's looking forward to when we will all join her, but she's not wallowing in self-pity because we're not there, or because she's not here. She's happy. I praise God for that.

I didn't share the vision with anyone for quite some time. It was too comforting, too awesome, so very holy that I didn't want anyone making fun of it or telling me it couldn't have happened or, that God doesn't work that way. It was a comforting reassurance that my precious Amy was all right. I savored that moment privately for a long time before I was brave enough to confess it to anyone.

Did you notice the sequence? First, God asked me to reaffirm my faith, then He sent comfort in the form of a vision. I believe the reaffirmation of my faith was necessary for me to be able to accept the vision as from God, for me to recognize His hand in it. He certainly could have sent the vision to me without reaffirming my faith. It was for my benefit, not His, that He asked me if I still believed in Him.

Chapter 6
Good Grief and Football…A Helping Vision

"One night the Lord spoke to Paul in a vision…"—Acts 18:9a

A couple of weeks after Art in the Park, God gave me another vision, one in which he showed me how he was helping me through my grief. One morning as I was waking up, I closed my eyes again, not quite ready to face the day. It was then that I saw the vision…a very dark image with black storm clouds in the sky. One light (a triangular one, like you might see in an old warehouse) was hanging down from heaven, emitting just enough light to see that I was on the one yard line of a horrible football field full of deep mud and muck. I was all alone on that field and wondered why. I figured it was because I held a special spot in grief as Amy's mother, but perhaps more importantly recognized that I was alone because no one else can truly feel what I'm feeling inside. No one. In that sense, I was alone.

But was I really alone? No. Thank God, no. In the next instant I saw a white ghost-like figure of a man to my left.

Somehow I knew he was the Holy Spirit; and he was with me to guide me through the sorrow, comfort me in my grief, and show me the way I needed to go in order to heal. In short, he was my coach and my guide. As long as I kept my eyes on him, we were making progress. However, the minute I turned my eyes away from him and started feeling sorry for myself (which I certainly did), he had to stop leading me in order to turn around and minister to me as I began to sink in the mud.

My eyes were then drawn to a dim light coming from the grandstands. As I looked that way, the light became brighter and I saw people standing up and cheering, just like they do at a football game. Without hearing their words, I knew their cheers were for me, beseeching our heavenly Father in my stead. "Give her some strength, Lord! Hold her in your arms and comfort her!" What amazed me was that whatever they prayed for was released to me and I was able to go on. Without their prayers I didn't have the strength nor the stamina to continue. Those prayer warriors were faithful, and I praise God for them. I could actually feel their prayers surrounding me, strengthening me and lifting me up.

That was all there was of the vision that morning, but it was enough to reach out for God's hand and have hope in his healing. He was helping me. What more could I possibly need?

Through the years there have been many revelations regarding my football game with God. Here are some of them:

I wrote about my daughter. First down. My husband and I reconnected while attending a class together. First down. You know what my faith-filled response was to these wonderful first downs? Big deal! What do I win with all this work and effort but the right to get up and do it again!? It usually takes many first downs before a touchdown is scored, and I figured I'd never make a touchdown until I died and rejoined my daughter in heaven. I decided, however, that it was better to get up and do it again instead of staying put and sinking in the mud.

From time to time I was blind-sided and tackled by something that reminded me of Amy and was overcome with grief again. Perhaps it was a favorite song of hers, or someone who reminded me of her. Whatever it was, I hadn't seen it coming, was thrown for a loss and had to fight my way back to where I had been.

Quite often I did the tackling. I tackled something I needed to do. Perhaps it was as simple as getting out of bed in the morning, but it required effort on my part. I tackled it. I didn't always want to, and didn't always succeed, but progress was made in the attempt.,

Receiving usually involved other "players" who had also lost children. There's an instant understanding between grieving parents, an understanding that doesn't even need words. We just know. They would pass understanding to me and I would be encouraged to go on. Their special understanding was vital to me. I appreciated the fact that I wasn't the only one to ever suffer like this, but at the same time wished none of us understood. The cost of understanding is too high.

At times I was privileged to throw a few passes of my own. By counseling other grieving parents, by listening to them, by sharing my story, I passed the ball of understanding to them. You see, in my heart, I needed to process what had happened over and over. I believe it helped both of us…the person I was talking to, and me.

A football player does not enter the football game without gear to protect him. It would be really stupid to do that. The same thing holds true in a spiritual football game. I needed to put on the entire armor of God in order to stand my ground (Check out Ephesians 6:11-18).

The shield of faith was especially helpful. When I was in my twenties, I chose I Thessalonians 5:18 as my life verse: "In all things give thanks, for this is the will of Christ Jesus in you." Well, let me tell you, giving thanks when you've just lost your daughter is terribly difficult. But the verse does not say "In all GOOD things." It says "In ALL things." It doesn't say "FOR all things" either. It says, "IN all things."

My task then was to look for things for which I could be truly thankful. And I do mean look. I'm thankful that Amy didn't suffer. I'm thankful God met her at her point of need, just as he is meeting me at mine. (I don't LIKE that point of need, but I'm thankful for his help.) I'm thankful for the visions he's given me, for the faithful prayer warriors, for all the people who have ministered to me and my family, for reconnecting with my husband, for help in getting Bob home, for the ability to fall asleep at night. For so many things I am truly grateful.

For a long time I didn't think I had possession of the ball. I was so numb. How could I possibly hold the ball too? I felt like a victim responding and struggling to cope with this horrible situation. But I DID have the ball! I had it because I had the power to decide what I was going to do. I didn't have to be a victim who could do absolutely nothing. I could cope. I could get better. I could fight the good fight. Granted, it wasn't easy, but I could put forth the effort.

I had thought touchdowns in this life were impossible in my situation. I would be making first downs for the rest of my life, but never a touchdown until I died and rejoined Amy in heaven. I was wrong.

Thank God I was wrong! The only touchdown I've ever made came about five years after the kick-off (the accident). Finally, finally, I entered my "new normal." I am now able to enjoy life again. I can honestly laugh, truly enjoy my friends, relish the presence of my loved ones, watch my grandbabies grow with delight in my heart. Yes… I wish Amy was here to enjoy it too. Yes… I miss her every day. And yes… I still want my "old normal" back. But the point is, I am ABLE to still enjoy life and I am ABLE to look forward to the future. That's an amazing healing.

What makes that possible is the fact that Jesus Christ died on the cross for me, for Amy, for my loved ones, for you. Because he paid for her ticket to heaven by beating death and rising again, I can look forward to seeing Amy again. I can look forward to hugging her, to spending FOREVER with her. The Bible tells us we will grieve. It's impossible to avoid that. BUT…it also says we will not grieve as those who have no hope. Because of what Jesus did on the cross, we HAVE hope. I am truly thankful for that!

Time outs are essential to my mental health. It is very difficult for me to attend church on Mother's Day. On that day, I take a time out from attending church. I'll go the night before, but not on Mother's Day. It's just too hard. I'm Amy's mother, and her grave is only several yards away from the church. It's too painful, especially with the contrast of everyone smiling and wishing me a Happy Mother's Day. Time outs serve a useful purpose, and it's o.k. to take them.

My coach (the Holy Spirit) is also a wonderful counselor. One evening my husband and I were watching a movie in which the mother unexplainably goes into a coma for 20 years. The daughter's name in the movie was Emma, which happened to be one of our pet names for Amy. (So much so that Amy included it as a middle name when she signed her name.)

Then one day the mother woke up. When her husband told Emma that something had happened to her mother, she quickly ran into her mom's bedroom for a tearful, joyful, radiant reunion. It was like sticking a knife in my heart. That wonderful reunion is one that I ache for and will never have in this world. I had to get up and leave the room. It was almost like losing my "Emma" all over again, only this time there was no numbness to protect me from the pain. I sobbed. After a day or two, the Lord said to me, "Someday that's going to be you."

That stopped me right in my tracks and made all the difference in the world to me. Someday I will have that wonderful reunion with my daughter! Someday I will see her again and joyfully hug her! I think we'll both be radiant on that day!

Changing my focus from the terrible pain of separation to the promised joy of that yearned for reunion was exactly what I needed. Does it still hurt right now? Of course. To tell the truth, there are still days when I want to stamp my foot and say, "I've had enough! I want her back, and I want her back now!" But…and notice this…I have forever to look forward to with my "Emma" because of what Jesus did on the cross for us. That is what takes the STING out of death. It still hurts, but the terribleness of it has been lifted. Joy in the midst of pain. Hope in the midst of sorrow.

All high school and college football teams have school songs. I, too, was given a song for my football game with God. It happened like this: While on vacation in Arizona, I thought of a long-ago memory of some high school boys singing their own version of an old WWII song. Part of their words were, "Football, football, my favorite game of the year. Football, football..." Wondering why in the world I was remembering that song (personally, I think the Holy Spirit brought it to mind), I looked the words up on the internet. These are some of the words I found:

> Although there are oceans we must cross
> And mountains that we must climb
> I know every game must have a loss
> So pray that our loss is nothing but time
> Till then, let's dream of what there will be
> Till then, we'll call on each memory
> Till then, when I will hold you again,
> Please wait, wait till then

Are those words applicable to my grief? Oh, yes! Crossing oceans and climbing mountains convey the message of great effort, of a struggle to overcome obstacles. "Every game must have a loss"...rather obvious. But then the next phrase... "Pray that our loss is nothing but time." Wow! That phrase gave me goose bumps. As long as Christ is our Savior, our loss IS nothing but time. We'll have forever to make up for what we've lost here and now. If he's not our savior, then the loss is forever. Wow.

God even gave me a poem for our football game. Officially I wrote it, but He inspired it, and so I really consider Him to be the author.

> Closing my eyes I wrap my arms around the air
> Pretending…pretending you're still there
> A little girl once more upon my lap
> Sharing love and laughter
>
> Whispering sweet nothings in your ear
> I softly place a kiss upon your head
> Only to open my eyes and find
> My heart's tears falling on your grave instead
>
> Amazed and awed I sense Christ's tears upon my heart
> Washing mine away with words of comfort, hope and love
> "Remember, oh remember my precious one
> My tears and drops of blood were shed for you."
>
> "Upon that cross I paid the price in full
> For you, and all your loved ones to redeem
> So that within heaven's gates you may rejoice
> Face to face again with those you love"
>
> "The sweet reunion yearned for awaits…your homecoming
> We'll welcome you with open arms
> It's a day we look forward to as well
> For at last…at last our loved one has come home"

"In peace and joy, oh precious one reside
In hope and love await the day
When heaven's glory surrounds your soul
And sweet reunions fill your heart again."

Vange Anderson, March, 2007

That poem is for you too. Can you just imagine being welcomed into heaven with open arms by people longing to see you?

Now, I've got to tell you…I don't have a death wish. I want to be here with my loved ones as long as possible. I have no wish to leave them nor do I ever want to cause them pain. However, if you're around when it is my time to go, please do an odd favor for me.

You're going to have to do it quietly, because if anyone hears you, they'll think you're nuts. Just walk up to my casket and quietly say with feeling, "You go, girl!" And then listen. You just might hear echoing down from the halls of heaven (or at least in the echoes of your mind), "Woo-hoo! Amy! Oh thank you, Jesus! Thank you Lord Jesus for making this possible!" What a wonderful Lord we serve!

You see, joy CAN live in the same body as grief, but only if Jesus Christ also resides there. Because of Him I can look forward to tomorrow. I can experience joy in the midst of my sorrow. The pain is there, but so is the hope. He can comfort, console, guide, call others to pray for you, inspire you with visions, songs, and whatever he chooses to use. He is able to change your focus and replace your despair with hope. And he loves to do it because He loves us so much. We just need to be open and willing to do what he asks of us.

Chapter 7
What Grief Is Like When You've Lost a Child

"You will grieve, but not like those who have no faith."
—I Thess. 4:13

Linda was like a soul mate to me. Whenever I called her up with a problem, she knew exactly what I was dealing with. She could do the same with me. She wanted to do the same with my grief, and believed she understood what I was dealing with. I couldn't convince her that this was different. It bothered me enough that several days later I wrote her a letter. This is part of that letter:. Dear Linda,

I'm writing this because I know you very well. You truly want to be a blessing to those who are mourning. If that were not true, I would not write this letter.

There are some things you don't fully understand because you have not walked that road yourself. You have not lost a child of your own. Losing a child is different from the loss of other loved ones. Even if you can understand and appreciate the loss to a great degree, it will be frustrating for most grieving parents to hear you express that, simply because they won't believe you. All of the grieving parents I've talked to, yes, all of them, are more comforted by those who extend their sympathy and admit, "I can't imagine." Because, to tell you the truth, grieving parents don't think you can.

Think of one person who has passed away, and answer all the questions with that one person in mind:

(I continued the letter by asking several questions such as:)

Since that person's death, has even one day gone by when you didn't think of them? Where were you and what were you doing when you first heard the news? What were the last words you had with your precious one? What is the color of the eyes of the person who told you your loved one had died?

Have you "been hit from your blind side," that is, suddenly been overcome with grief again…and you didn't see it coming? When and how did that happen to you? How do you deal with the pain that is always just below the surface?

What sorts of pain did you feel in your body? Did you have any breathing problems, any problems with memory? Weight loss or gain? Trouble focusing? Sleeping problems? Numbness? Did you ever wonder why the world was still moving?

Which holiday is the most difficult for you to get through? Have you changed any holiday traditions? Are there any days that are difficult for you to sit through a church service? Why do you think that is?

How do you grieve your loss and still try to make others feel your love for them? What do you do to honor your loved one during holidays and special events? How are your family gatherings different now? How do you deal with that?

How did your relationship with your spouse change? Name one time when your needs collided—when his needs were different from yours, and both could not be met. How did you cope with that?

How well were you able to communicate with each other about your loss? Did that cause hurt? How did you get past that? Are you past that? Do you need to go to someone other than your spouse to receive understanding for what you're dealing with?

What do you do when you see someone who resembles your precious one? Do you ever find yourself looking at people— the backs of their heads, their profiles, and think they "sort of" resemble your dear one and it's a blessing because that's almost like seeing them alive again?

Have you ever missed the person so much that your eyes and ears actually ached with the desire to see and hear him or her again? Have you ever prayed with all your heart to dream about them so you could at least "see" them that way or "feel" their presence?

Have you ever found yourself in a store with tears welling up in your eyes because you see something your loved one would have enjoyed? Do you ever buy yourself a gift because it's something they would have picked up for you?

Do you ever say your precious one's name out loud when no one else is around, just to hear the sound of it? How often do you ask the Lord to tell your loved one that you love them?

Have you ever bought special frames to put their pictures in to remind you they're in God's loving care? Have you done something special for their grave? What about where they died?

Did you do anything special with something that belonged to him or her? Have you volunteered anywhere because you know they would be proud of you for doing that, or because it was something they either struggled with or were gifted with?

Have you ever bought something for a needy person that you would have loved buying for your loved one?

That was the main part of the letter. Several days later I received a call from Linda. She said, "You're right...there were so many things I would never have thought of. I'm going to keep this forever. It should be published so others can understand too." She believed it would help her minister to others more effectively. I hope that is true for you as well.

Chapter 8
Forgiveness

"And when ye stand praying, forgive, if you have aught against any; that your Father also which is in heaven may forgive you your trespasses, But if ye do not forgive, neither will your Father which is in heaven forgive your trespasses."
—Mark 11:25-26

Not only is forgiveness a requirement for us to be forgiven, it is a major step in the healing process. You won't heal very well if you have the poison of unforgiveness in your soul. Forgiveness isn't easy. Some people may not even deserve to be forgiven. The point is, however, that you deserve and need to be rid of the poison that unforgiveness brings.

A fifteen-year-old girl was driving the car when our Amy died. Even though she ran as fast as she could to get help, it was too late. Our Amy was already gone. Even if we had been following the car, there's nothing we could have done to save her.

Causing the death of a friend is a horrible thing for a 15-year-old girl (or anyone) to carry with her the rest of her life. And we knew our Amy well enough to know she would want us to assure her friend of our forgiveness and desire to help her heal.

It was for Amy that I went through the motions. A day or two after the accident my husband and I went to her friend's home to assure her of the fact that we did not blame her. She didn't cause the accident on purpose. It's not called an "on purpose" for a reason. Even though she could have done things differently (couldn't we all!?), it was an accident, a terrible one, but an accident nonetheless.

That visit was crucial to the girl's healing, and ours. We didn't realize how important God's timing was until a few days after the funeral. The entire family left the state without telling anyone they were leaving. The morning we went to see Amy's friend was the only opportunity we had to minister to her.

A few months later we received a letter. In it she expressed her appreciation for what we had done, and stated that she was getting counseling. She went on to say we were a big reason she was doing as well as she was. And I might add, a reason we were doing as well as we were.

We knew Amy would be proud of us. The autumn before the accident, she had written an essay about a mother who had been killed by a drunk driver. The daughter in her story had to work through forgiveness, learned to forgive the driver, who then had the hope and drive to make something better out of his life. I knew, without a doubt, that Amy would want us to assure her friend that we did not blame her.

When we forgive, we prevent anger and bitterness from

taking root in our hearts. It's one of the reasons we are told in the Bible not to let the sun go down on our anger: ("Even if you are angry, you must not sin; never let the sun set on your anger or else you will give the devil a foothold…" (Ephesians 4:26-27). Anger is understandable, it's just not healthy or good for the person who lets it smolder in their mind and heart.

Sometimes we need to work very hard at forgiving. Losing a child through intentional violence would be so much more difficult to forgive. I can't imagine that. I only know the One who can, the One who can help all of us walk through forgiveness.

I do remember going through a very difficult time of forgiving many years ago. I had to forgive my ex-husband for, among other things, moving in with his girlfriend. Forgiveness in that case took years. At one point I had to admit to my Lord, "I'm not willing to forgive, but I'm willing to be made willing." God worked on my heart and my will. Little by little I was able to let go of the bitterness and forgive him. It was not easy. At times I would think, "Okay, I've worked through it. I'm done forgiving him." Then something would happen and I would have to work through it all over again from another angle. It took a long, long time. The peace at the end was worth every minute of the struggle.

Why is it worth the struggle? Because forgiving others opens the door to peace. As my grandmother used to say, Un-"Forgiveness is a sword. There is more poison in the handle than in the blade." Not forgiving someone is like carrying that person around on your back every minute of every angry day. You're thinking about the pain he caused you, what a dirty rotten thing he did, what a terrible person he is, and the fact that he doesn't deserve to be forgiven. The trouble with that is, he's not the one who's feeling the pain...you are. He may feel no pain whatsoever. You see? More poison in the handle than in the blade.

Do YOURSELF a favor. Forgive. Your Father in Heaven will bless you with His peace. It is worth going for! I can tell you that from experience.

Chapter 9
Things Others Did That Helped

"Treat others as you would like them to treat you."
—Luke 6:31

We are blessed to live in a rural community where neighbors are in the habit of helping one another. If a farmer is too sick to do his work, the neighbors get together and do it for him. When someone loses a loved one, the neighbors come armed with casseroles, bars, or whatever to help.

Our house became like a train station for three days. There was a constant flow of people in and out offering their love and support. My sister Kathy remarked that that would never have happened in the city, where she lives. Probably not. But don't let that stop you from offering your support. Perhaps you'll wake your neighborhood up to actually care for one another.

Here are some of the things that helped:

1. People came. It began in the trauma room when dear ones heard about the accident and came running in. It continued

when we arrived home to find out neighbor Bruce and Pastor Mark waiting to hug us. For three days it continued, reminding us of the love and prayers that were being offered up on our behalf. It was consoling to know that people were standing with us.

2. People brought a variety of things. Casseroles, all kinds of bars and cookies, some things I would never have thought of. My sister-in-law Sue came in with toilet paper! And we needed it! I'll never forget one of the high school teachers walking into our kitchen armed with ready-to-bake pizzas. They never did make it to the freezer. Our children grabbed them and baked them right away. It was a love token that spoke to them! Since then, if we know there are children in the home, we bring pizza.

3. People came several days later to retrieve their dishes. It saved me from having to go to all their homes to return the dishes that were here. Others did not come and that was okay too. I was able to return them later. The only problem that came up were with unmarked dishes and trays. If there had been names on the dishes, they were gone. One was a brand new angel food cake pan. I was never able to return it. I didn't know who it belonged to.

4. Our dear neighbor, Dick, came for our dirty towels, brought them home to wash, and then returned them. I never saw him come, and he never mentioned it to me. To this day he has not mentioned it. I only know about it because our children told me. A few days after the accident I looked out our front window, and there was Dick, mowing our lawn. He never said anything about that, either. And I thought what an example of Christian service he was. He didn't do it for recognition or honor, he just did it to serve. How Christ-like.

5. Neighbors brought other things…. a tent with no sides so people could sit out of the sun…a tape of Christian music, an angel figurine talking on the phone with the saying, "Hi Mom. I love you", an angel lamp, an engraved gold locket with Amy's picture in it, a cross and wild flower seeds for the accident site. The list goes on…

6. Silent hugs. That may seem like a strange thing to you, but it really helped. For me the silent hugs became like prayers of the Holy Spirit. We're told he prays for us in groans too deep for mere words to express (Romans 8:26). That's what my pain was like…too deep to express in mere words…but it was somehow expressed in the silent hugs because the Holy Spirit was also there. Sometimes the best gift you can give IS your silent presence. Just BEING there is a wonderful support. The fact that you cared enough to come into a difficult situation where you didn't know what to say speaks volumes. There is a connection in that kind of silence…an appreciation for your presence…and even an appreciation for your silence. For it is then we know your heart hurts enough that you don't know how to express it…but your silent concerned presence DOES express it. Please remember that.

7. Maid Service. Some dear ladies came every day to wash dishes, make coffee, sweep the floor, whatever needed to be done. One of them didn't even know me at the time, but she is now a dear friend. They came every day until after the funeral.

8. Scrap-booking: My friend Wendy spent a couple of long days at our house. She and my sister Kathy worked together to create a scrapbook about Amy. It's beautiful. We shared their work of love at Amy's funeral. It is still a treasure.

9. Music: While we arranged the music for the funeral, we were gifted by the women of our choir who just showed up to sing and play their violins. I was too numb to think of asking them to do that. They just did it in love. Some people gave us CD's of Christian music. That blessed us too.

10. Food at church: A dear one at church called the other members to ask them to bring food for the funeral. There's no way I could have planned any of that.

11. Written memories: On cards and letters people wrote about memories of Amy. The funny ones helped move me from sadness to happy memories. The tender ones gave me a glimpse of what my daughter was like away from home. I treasure those words and have often re- read them.

12. Etc. I don't know what else I'm forgetting, but use your gifts and talents to serve those who are grieving. I was told about a man who silently came in and polished all the shoes, of another who just came in and silently sat…both were somehow able to minister in their silence.

13. As a recap: Do go. Do say you're sorry. Do hug. Don't say you understand their grief. Don't try to explain their loss away. It's that simple.

Chapter 10
Good Intentions

"For the word of God is quick…. and is a discerner of the thoughts and intents of the heart."—Hebrews 4:12

We all need to realize that most people have good intentions, even when they say things that frustrate us. After church one day, I met a young mother holding her newborn. She tried to tell me how she truly understood my grief. I beg your pardon, but how in the world could she understand? She was holding her precious one. I had lost my precious one. She had not lost her child, she was holding her in her arms. My arms were empty. I was tempted to say, "Honey, you don't have a clue," but I didn't. Biting my tongue (and going in later for stitches…just kidding), I allowed her to have her say before I made my escape. Bless her heart, she was truly trying to give me solace and I had to honor her for that.

While knowing she did not truly understand, I had to appreciate her effort and know that her intentions were good. She may have had a point of reference, maybe even a strong point of reference, but she had not experienced the intensity of the actual event, and so was not successful in her heart-felt effort to console.

Unless you have actually lost a child of your own, avoid proclaiming your ability to understand, and thank your God that you can't even imagine. Because to tell you the truth, you can't; and those who have lost children hope you never find out.

People will say things without thinking.

About a year after the accident a gentleman asked me, "Well, are you over it yet?" I don't think so! Again God provided the grace to be gracious. I simply replied, "This isn't like a broken leg that heals and is as good as new. It's more like diabetes. You have to learn a new way of living with it." He said, "You're absolutely right." He meant well, and I needed to remind myself of that fact…even as I went home shaking my head in disbelief.

Some people, like me, want to talk about it. I need to process it over and over; so talking to me about it is fine. Others don't want to talk about it. My husband does not talk about it very often. It's too painful. I can understand that as well. Try to figure out what a person wants, whether they want to talk about it or not. If they do, listen. Ask questions or make loving comments if they seem appropriate. Treat them with care and concern. Don't dismiss their grief as if they should ever get over it. If you're not comfortable talking, send a card from time to time. Knowing others remember your loved one is a blessing.

Chapter 11
Clashing Needs

"…for your Father knoweth what things ye have need of, before ye ask him."—Matthew 6:8

As I mentioned before, grieving people will have different needs from one another. Some, like me, will want to talk about it. Others (like my husband) won't. I need to talk about and process my grief, he needs to compartmentalize, to put it away and get busy with other things. It's too painful for him to talk about. It's too painful for me not to talk about. This is a major reason many marriages fail after the loss of a child. There will come a time when your needs clash. It's that simple. Both will have important needs, but it will be impossible to meet both of them at the same time.

Our county fair occurred the month after Amy died. She had often served there at our church's food booth with us. My husband needed to be there to serve in her memory. I needed not to go near the place, but I needed him to stay with me. He went. I didn't.

The pain I felt that afternoon could be described as the lowest point following the funeral. Smiling would have been impossible for my face to do. I felt not only bereaved but abandoned and rejected. I couldn't stay home; I couldn't go to the fair. I didn't want to be with anyone. I didn't want to even be anywhere. I didn't even want to talk...I couldn't. I ended up driving to the lake and just sat by a tree close to the shore, hoping no one would recognize me. I simply wanted to disappear...to be oblivious to what was happening...to not recognize anything or anyone. I had a book in my hands, but I can't tell you what it was or what I read. I only know I had it so people would think I was lost in my book and wouldn't bother me.

I don't know how long I sat near that beach. It felt like a very long time, long enough to think that perhaps Dick would be home when I arrived there. He wasn't.

When he did come home we were silent for quite some time. Finally, I said, "You know when you needed to go to the fair and I didn't?" His body stiffened, as if ready for an assault. But this time, God gave me the grace I needed so that when he replied, "Yeah?" I simply said, "Well, I just needed you. I guess our needs were just too different." His body relaxed then, and any anger and frustration that might have been there disappeared. There was still a distance between us, but the fight had been defused. Thanks be to God. God knew I needed the grace to be non-combative. He graciously gave it to me.

It is at the point of clashing needs that so many marriages fail following the loss of a child. Hurt feelings and resentment are easily rooted in minds and hearts at times like those. Feelings of abandonment and indifference to your needs are imagined hurdles that need to be overcome if your marriage is to survive. It could have happened to us so easily. I had to remind myself over and over that he still loved me. His needs were different from mine, that's all. I needed to recognize that his needs were just as important as mine. It didn't feel that way, but they were.

The need to recognize Dick's needs as well as my own reminded me of my football game with God. Have you ever seen a football team win a game they were not determined to win? I mean really determined to win? I had to be determined to make our marriage work. I had to be determined to take whatever step God wanted me to take next. I needed to put as much effort into it as a determined football player puts into his game. Determination is needed to persevere when the going gets tough. I'm not going to win the game without it. Determination is that important, and it's something we can work on with God's help. (He'll give you the strength and motivation to persevere.)

We did not give up on our marriage. To be sure, there were some rough spots, but we did not give in. We were determined to stay together. Today we have a strong relationship again. We've been married for over 30 years, and he's still the neatest guy I've ever met. Perfection's not coming any time soon, but we're a team, and we love each other. (Remember, love is a decision, not a feeling.)

Chapter 12
Applying the Vision to Other Things

"A man's heart deviseth his way;
but the Lord directeth his steps."—Proverbs 16:9

The concepts presented in this book can be applied to many different situations: job changes, relationship problems, anxiety struggles, whatever. Compare your progress to first downs, your struggles to tackles, your success to touchdowns.

The basic step is to make sure the Holy Spirit is your coach and your guide. He can and will shine light on the next step he has for you, bring you comfort and hope, awaken your prayer warriors to pray. Keep your eyes on Him and you'll make progress. Take your eyes off of him, and it will be more difficult.

We're told that faith can move mountains (Matthew 21:21). Grief has been a huge mountain for me. It was (and sometimes still is) too overwhelming, too steep, and too huge to get over, around or under. It was only with God's help that I've been able to work through it. It's only with his love and help that I'm as well as I am. Whatever mountain you're dealing with, let the Holy Spirit help you. He's waiting for your permission.

Talk your situation over with the Lord; he will direct your path, showing you what to do next. May He bless you as you talk to him!

Chapter 13
Relationship with the Lord

"I will dwell in them and walk in them; and I will be their God and they shall be my people."—2 Corinthians 6:16b

We all know people who have lost children, or at least know of them. Some seem to heal after a time and are able to resume fairly normal lives. To be sure, they're never "the same," but they are able to enjoy life. Others seem to remain in their grief and after awhile become bitter, and are full of anger. They may not always speak of it, but it's there. You can almost feel it. What's the difference? Why do some make progress in the healing process and others don't?

Every time I've looked into it, parents who are better know Christ. The ones that aren't better, don't have a relationship with Him. It's like that bumper sticker declares,

No Christ, No Peace
Know Christ, Know Peace

It's that simple. It's all about relationship. It's not just a Sunday morning nod of acquaintance, it's a vital relationship of love and concern. When we lost Amy God didn't just stand idly by and say, "Oops." He was in the midst of it, ministering to our Amy and to us. While He welcomed Amy home with open arms, He was also comforting us…but more than just comforting us… He was hurting with us. Did you get that? HE was hurting with us. That amazes me, but it makes so much sense!

Whenever you've gone to a funeral, there's been a sense of hurt in you for those who are mourning. How much more so for our God who loved us enough to allow His Son to die for us. If He allowed that (and He did), then He's got to love us enough to hurt when we hurt. I hurt whenever any of my children hurt, and as God's children, He in turn hurts for us.

This truth is expressed beautifully by the words of a song written by Benjamin Gaither and Marshall Hall entitled "When I Cry":

When I Cry

Makin' a list of all of the good things
You've done for me Lord I've never been one to complain
But right now I'm lost, And I can't find my way
My world's come apart, And it's breaking my heart
But it helps to know that Your heart is breaking too

When I cry, You cry, When I hurt, You hurt
And when I've lost someone, it takes a piece of you too
When I fall on my face, You fill me with grace
Cause nothing breaks Your heart
Or tears You apart like when I cry

Alone in the dark, Face in my hands, crying out to You
Lord, there's never been a time in my life
There's so much at stake. There's so much to lose
But I trust it to You, You'll bring me through
And it helps me to know that I'm not alone

When I cry, You cry, When I hurt, You hurt
And when I've lost someone, it takes a piece of you too
When I fall on my face, You fill me with grace
Cause nothing breaks Your heart
Or tears You apart like when I cry

You're the one who calmed the raging sea
You're the one who made the blind to see
You looked through all of Heaven and eternity
And through it all, You saw me

When I cry, You cry, When I hurt, You hurt
And when I've lost someone, it takes a piece of you too
When I fall on my face, You fill me with grace
Cause nothing breaks Your heart
Or tears You apart like when I cry Mmmm....

Chapter 14
Things That Help You

*"Enter into his gates with thanksgiving and into his courts
with praise; be thankful unto him and bless his name."*
—Psalms 100:4

I've come to think of praise and thanksgiving as not only the
manner in which we are to enter God's courts, but as keys to his
kingdom. Using praise and thanksgiving give us access to him. I
used to wonder about this. Didn't our Lord say that he was with
us always? (Matthew 28:20). Why did I have to give him thanks
and praise in order to enter his kingdom then? I'm still not sure of
the answer, but I think it has more to do with us being aware that
we have entered his kingdom, that we are indeed in God's
presence. Praising and thanking God then, are actually gifts for us.

1. Give thanks and praise to God.
Look for things that you can honestly be thankful for and
thank God for them. Consider the praise-worthy qualities of
God and praise him for them.

2. Recognize and remind yourself of God's ministering hand to you through other people.

3. Ask God what he wants you to learn through this. What is he trying to tell you?

4. Relate your progress to football.

A. The Holy Spirit is your coach and your guide.

B. The cheering section is made up of prayer warriors for you.

C. First Downs: What have you done to earn a first down in your situation?

D. Tackling: How have you been tackled and how did you fight your way back to where you had been? How did you tackle things on your agenda that were a bit difficult?

E. Passing: How did others help you by "passing" along encouragement and/or assistance? How did you help others with what you have learned through your experience?

F. Possession of the ball: Do you feel you have possession of the ball? What are you able to decide? Does that mean you have at least possession of the ball at times?

G. Football gear: Put on the full armor of God (see Ephesians 6:11-18)

H. Touchdowns: When you make a significant aim, consider it as a touchdown.

I. Etc.

5. Remember and read verses that apply to your situation.

A. Use a concordance. If you don't have one, buy one. A concordance is a reference book that gives you chapter and verse for various topics. (example: strengthened, Ephesians 3:16)

B. Memorize and repeat meaningful verses to yourself.
C. Have pictures of Christ, etc.

6. Remember what you've been taught as a Christian.
   A. God's love
   B. How Christ purchased your ticket to heaven.
   C. He meets us at our need.

7. Ask for prayer support.

8. Saturate yourself spiritually.
   A. Read the Bible.
   B. Listen to Christian radio, watch Christian movies, read Christian books.
   C. Pray
   D. Write a letter to God: write his responses. Check to make sure it agrees with His Word (the Bible).

9. Remember men and women often grieve differently.
   A. Anticipate a time when your needs will collide. How will you handle it?
   B. Ask God for insight into how you should think and act.

10. Remember your loved one...
    A. Do something with things that belonged to your loved one.... frame them, preserve and give them to someone who loved them, etc.
    B. Journal about them...what was special about them, how you felt about them, etc.

C. Buy yourself gifts that your loved one would have bought for you.

11. Check your attitude. The belief that you can get better and, that you can make progress is vital.

12. Dedicate your day to the Lord in the morning. Ask him to help you be the person he wants you to be for that day. (The person he wants you to be for your husband, friend, etc)

13. Be kind to yourself. When you blow it, forgive yourself and try again. You're human, and it's ok.

14. Plan ahead. What are you going to do to get through significant anniversaries. How will you honor your loved one on that day?
   A. Do something for someone else in their memory
   B. Pray, visit their grave, etc.
   C. Do something that they enjoyed...
      • I drink a Cherry Pepsi because it was my daughter's favorite.
      • We light fireworks off because buying fireworks was one of the last things we did together.
      • Provide funds for a needy person to do what your loved one would have enjoyed.
      • Her friend eats a tuna sandwich in her honor

Chapter 15
Closure

The root of our healing, of course, is a close relationship with our Lord and Savior, Jesus Christ. He's the one who brings the understanding and encouragement that is so vital, the One who sends the Holy Spirit to be our coach and our guide. He reminds us of songs, inspires poems, whispers encouragement to us in the dark. Keep your eyes on Him and you'll make progress. Take your eyes off Him, and your journey will be more difficult.

We're told that faith can move mountains. Grief is a mountain that seems too overwhelming, too steep, and too huge. But with Christ, all things are possible. He will take you THROUGH it. It takes time, faith, hope, work, determination and perseverance, but it IS possible.

Thank you, dear reader, for spending this time with me. You are in my thoughts and prayers. My prayer is that God will bring you through whatever you're dealing with, so that you may experience his love for you and know him as your Lord and Savior. We'll have forever to get acquainted in Heaven! I'm looking forward to that! My prayer for you:

Oh, Father God, when we lost Amy we asked you to get every drop of good you could possibly get from it because it was costing us so much. I'm asking you to continue raining that drop of good down on each person reading this book. Give them the understanding, hope, joy and love that you want to give them. Remind them of the teachings you want them to remember so they will find the hope and peace that only you can give. Thank you for loving us with the love that passes understanding, and giving us joy in the midst of our pain. You are an awesome God. Thank you so much for allowing us to know and serve you. For it is in your name I pray. Amen.